# Lighten Up!

# Lighten Up!
## 100 Funny Little Poems

Edited by Bruce Lansky

**Meadowbrook Press**

Distributed by Simon & Schuster
New York

Library of Congress Cataloging-in-Publication Data
Lighten up!/selected by Bruce Lansky.
p. cm.
ISBN 0-671-31632-X (Simon & Schuster)
ISBN 0-88166-320-4 (Meadowbrook)
1. Humorous poetry, American. I. Lansky, Bruce.
PS595.H8L58 1998
811'.0708—dc21
98-8788
CIP

Editor: Bruce Lansky
Coordinating Editor: Heather Hooper
Production Manager: Joe Gagne
Production Assistant: Danielle White

© 1998 by Meadowbrook Creations

Published by Meadowbrook Press, 5451 Smetana Drive; Minnetonka,
Minnesota 55343

BOOK TRADE DISTRIBUTION by Simon & Schuster, a division of Simon
and Schuster, Inc., 1230 Avenue of the Americas, New York, NY 10020

02 01 00     10 9 8 7 6 5 4 3

Printed in the United States of America

# Acknowledgments

We would like to thank John Mella, editor of *Light,* the only magazine in the United States devoted solely to light verse, for his advice and assistance in contacting a number of talented light verse writers.

We would like to thank the individuals who served on a reading panel for this project:

Margerie Goggin Allen, Bruce Bennett, Laurel Blossom, Karen Brown, Dorothy Brummel, Mary Margaret Carlisle, Faye W. Click, Edmund Conti, Pat D'Amico, Dr. Alfred Dorn, Dr. Robert N. Feinstein, Henry G. Fischer, David Galef, Charles L. Grove, William Harmon, Dick Hayman, Paul Humphrey, Felicia Lamport, Jo. S. Kittinger, Sydnie Meltzer Kleinhenz, Helen Ksypka, Katherine McAlpine, Charlene Meltzer, Richard Moore, Lois Muehl, Sheryl L. Nelms, Kenn Nesbitt, Bruce E. Newling, Richard Nickson, Leslie D. Perkins, Charles W. Pratt, Rockin' Red, Joan Drew Ritchings, Jerry Rosen, Mae Scanlan, Lawrence Schimel, Robert Scotellaro, Ernest Slyman, Albert Sterback, Denise Tiffany, Timothy Tocher, Esther Towns, Mary Veazy, Evelyn Amuedo Wade, Stan Werlin, Gail White, Zira Wood, Dina Wren

# Table of Contents

This book contains the wittiest, most entertaining poems I could find. If I've done my job well, you'll find it almost impossible to finish this book without a smile on your face.

And, if this book makes you smile, I hope you'll spread the word by sharing your favorite funny little poems: read the poems aloud, stick them on your refrigerator, pin them to your office bulletin board, write them on your blackboard, quote them in conversation and in letters, read them at open-mike poetry events at bookstores and coffee shops.

I'm always happy to discover that people who usually don't like poetry thoroughly enjoy the poems in this book. I suppose that changing people's minds about poetry was almost as strong a reason for publishing this book as making people smile.

*Bruce Lansky*

# Here's to Light Verse

I am sorry to say many poets today
Simply frown upon meter and rhyming;
They tend to immerse their muse in free verse
Without any humor or timing.

In line after line it is hard to divine
Their nebulous phrasing or musing;
Whose meanings escape me and metaphors drape me
In boredom conducive to snoozing.

Oh where are the rhymes and the whimsy of times
That gave us a Nash or a Parker?
They are not, it is clear, where they used to appear
in *The* (once celebrated) *New Yarker.*

Some critics have said that light verse is dead
And readers are well beyond caring;
You would think it had fleas or some dreadful disease
Too risky for touching or sharing.

So let me explain that critics disdain
Any muse that's not purely aesthetic;
Since light verse ain't dead, they would have us instead,
Consider the stuff unpoetic.

Yet that, I decree, doesn't sit well with me,
Nor does it deter my ambition;
For I'd rather create than deflect or deflate
Verse to lighten the human condition.

*—Ned Pastor*

# General Review of the Sex Situation

Woman wants monogamy;
Man delights in novelty.
Love is woman's moon and sun;
Man has other forms of fun.
Woman lives but in her lord;
Count to ten, and man is bored.
With this the gist and sum of it,
What earthly good can come of it?

—*Dorothy Parker*

## Tennyson Anyone?

In the spring a young man's fancy
lightly turns to thoughts of love;
And in summer,
and in autumn,
and in winter—
See above.

*—E. Y. Harburg*

## Touching Moments

They say that love is always blind
And that explains so much—
Young lovers always seem so prone
To use their sense of touch.

—*Charles Ghigna*

## Inscriptions on a Lipstick

Oh, innocent victims of Cupid,
Remember this terse little verse;
To let a fool kiss you is stupid,
To let a kiss fool you is worse.

—*E. Y. Harburg*

## Scrambled

I climbed up the door
And I opened the stairs.
I said my pajamas
And buttoned my prayers.

I turned off the covers
And pulled up the light.
I'm all scrambled up since
She kissed me last night.

*—adapted by Bruce Lansky*

## Unfortunate Coincidence

By the time you swear you're his,
    Shivering and sighing,
And he vows his passion is
    Infinite, undying—
Lady, make a note of this:
One of you is lying.

—*Dorothy Parker*

## Flower Power

My true love brought me flowers tonight,
And I'm all smiles and song.
I guess I'm doing something right—
Or he's done something *wrong!*

—*Maureen Cannon*

# We'd Been Apart for Many Years

We'd been apart for many years,
Then met one day by chance.
I hoped we might rekindle
The flame of our romance.

But we could neither touch nor speak,
The fates conspired to spite us,
For she had poison ivy,
and I had laryngitis.

—*Jack Prelutsky*

# I Worry

I worry about you—
So long since we spoke.
Love, are you downhearted,
Dispirited, broke?

I worry about you.
I can't sleep at night.
Are you sad? Are you lonely?
Or are you all right?

They say that men suffer,
As badly, as long.
I worry, I worry,
In case they are wrong.

—*Wendy Cope*

# Room Temperature

Some hoist the windows, gasp for air,
    While others find it chilly.
Some turn up thermostats a hair,
    While others think them silly.

Some like it cold, some like it hot,
    Some freeze, while others smother.
And by some fiendish, fatal plot
    They marry one another.

—*Richard Armour*

## A Word to Husbands

To keep your marriage brimming,
With love in the loving cup,
Whenever you're wrong, admit it;
Whenever you're right, shut up.

—*Ogden Nash*

# Lucky Dilemma

I'd send her sweets to celebrate,
But damn those dental bills!
Most flowers make me hesitate—
Her allergy needs pills.

The jewelry I bring home won't do,
She doesn't share my taste;
High fashion for a lady who
Loves jeans is just a waste.

I cannot send a VCR,
She's not TV-inclined.
Why buy a lovely objet d'art?
My dear is colorblind!

An island cruise has no appeal—
Choppy seas upset her;
And fear of flying's an ordeal
That isn't any better.

Selecting gifts is just *de trop*.
Still, I'm a lucky gent:
For unlike other wives I know,
Mine seldom costs a cent!

—*Ned Pastor*

## The Perfect Mate

You're handsome and funny.
You're charming and kind.
Your body is stunning,
And so is your mind.

Your talents are many.
Your wardrobe is great.
But nothing surpasses
Your taste in a mate.

—*Ellen Jackson*

## Midlife Muddle

When we were young, you made me blush,
go hot and cold, and turn to mush.
I still feel all these things, it's true . . .
but is it menopause, or you?

—*Susan D. Anderson*

## Past Perfect

Wives delight in telling wives
Of the moment in their lives
When, though not exactly lonely,
Bang! they met their one and only.

Husbands, though, among their pals,
Speak more often of the gals
Whom they gave impassioned kisses
Long before they met the Mrs.

—*Richard Armour*

## Tit for Tat

My paring knife, he would often use
For opening cans or turning screws.
Nor would he listen to my complaint
Till I used his chisel for stirring paint.

—*Ruth E. Lancaster*

### Careless Talk

Bill
Was ill.

In his delirium
He talked about Miriam.

This was an error
As his wife was a terror

Known
As Joan.

—*Mark Hollis*

## Marriage Couplet

I think of my wife, and I think of Lot,
And I think of the lucky break he got.

—*William Rossa Cole*

## Miniature

My day-old son is plenty scrawny,
His mouth is wide with screams, or yawny,
His ears seem larger than his needing.
His nose is flat, his chin receding,
His skin is very, very red,
He has no hair upon his head,
And yet I'm proud as proud can be
To hear you say he looks like me.

—*Richard Armour*

## On Watching Your Friend Trying to Make Her Baby Drink from a Cup for the First Time

Sip a little
Sup a little
From your little
Cup a little
Sup a little
Sip a little
Put it to your
Lip a little

Tip a little
Tap a little
Not into your
Lap or it'll
Drip a little
Drop a little
On the table
Top a little!

—*James Kirkup*

# Ninth Month Inventory

We have a silk-lined bassinet;
We have two kinds of cribs
(One portable, one stay-at-home);
We have a hundred bibs.

We have a thousand diapers and
We have a rocking chair;
We have a tiny comb in case
The baby has some hair.

We have a baby carriage and a
Car seat and a swing;
We have twelve baby bottles and a
Prechilled teething ring.

We have ten books on baby care and
Parenting techniques;
We have six rubber lap pads just in
Case the baby leaks.

We have three closets full of sheets
And blankets, towels, and clothes;
We have a baby-sized syringe for
Cleaning out the nose.

We have a yellow rubber duck;
We have a soft brown teddy;
We have eleven charge cards just in
Case we're still not ready.

—*Leslie Danford Perkins*

## Where's the Baby?

Our brand-new baby is so small,
He's hardly even there at all.
The only way that we can find him
Is by the smell he leaves behind him.

—*Bruce Lansky*

# The Difference Is . . .

First-time parents never miss
    A single tiny feat.
They film it, note it in The Book,
    And shout it in the street:
"He smiled today! Had four BMs!
    He spit up on the cat!
He got a tooth! He slept all night—
    Can you imagine that?"

But second-timers note the facts
    And take each one in stride:
"He's learned to take his diaper off—
    You'd better step aside."

—*Babs Bell Hajdusiewicz*

## The Pickle Jar

Thank goodness for the pickle jar,
  A standard feature in our car.
When sons have signaled they must go,
  And traffic's jammed or lights are slow,
our handy-dandy pickle jar
  Relieves the tension where we are.
I can't imagine what folks do
  When daughters need to potty, too.

—*Sydnie Meltzer Kleinhenz*

## Please Graduate!

Get in and study, Junior, please,
    And skip a grade or two.
Though I'm not fond of prodigies,
    I cherish your I.Q.

Obey the teacher, break no rule,
    And speed the blessed day
When you will graduate from school
    And I from P.T.A.

—*Richard Armour*

## College Bills

The bill from college came today
For all our children's fees;
As parents we are doomed to grow
much poorer by degrees.

—*Charles Ghigna*

## Student Away

Dear daughter in that distant dorm,
I can see your sprawling form,
The scattered textbooks, notes, swirled smoke,
Candy wrappers, cans of Coke.

At home your room now rests serene,
Desk uncluttered, ashtrays clean.
And darling, though for you I pine,
This arrangement suits me fine.

—*Martha H. Freedman*

## Rerun

Our children inform us of wonderful things,
Things that they feel we should know;
Forgetting that those were the very same things
We taught them ourselves long ago.

—*Evelyn Amuedo Wade*

## Nurses Nurse

Nurses nurse
And teachers teach
And tailors mend
And preachers preach
And barbers trim
And chauffeurs haul
And parents get to do it all.

—*Babs Bell Hajdusiewicz*

# Proof of the Puppy

He sharpened his teeth
    On the legs of the table
And left, on the rug,
    His indelible label.

He tested his claws
    On the arms of the chair
And deep in the sofa
    Deposited hair.

And now that he's grown,
    As I frequently grouse,
We've a house-broken dog
    And a dog-broken house.

*—Richard Armour*

## Even Fast Learners Make Mistakes

I taught my dog to fetch my shoes,
She learned how in a minute,
but brought back a size thirteen
With someone's foot still in it.

—*Gene Fehler*

## My Dog

My dog is such a gentle soul,
Although he's big it's true.
He brings the paper in his mouth.
He brings the postman too.

—*Max Fatchen*

## The Dog

The truth I do not stretch or shove
When I state the dog is full of love.
I've also proved, by actual test,
A wet dog is the lovingest.

—*Ogden Nash*

# Watchdog

We bought him for a watchdog
　　But he mixes up his ends:
He wags his tail at strangers,
　　And barks at all our friends.

We got him for protection,
　　We thought he'd earn his keep.
But he frightens little children—
　　When he isn't fast asleep.

He's very fond of hoboes
　　And gypsies and the like,
But nips the friendly postman
　　And the newsboy on his bike.

He causes feuds and lawsuits,
　　He keeps us tense and grim . . .
We bought him for a watchdog,
　　But *we* keep watch on *him*.

## —Richard Armour

# Poorly Dressed

I have a friend who's not well dressed.
He wears no hat. He wears no vest.

Upon his back he wears no shirt,
So you can see there's lots of dirt.

He wears no shoes upon his feet.
He wears no pants upon his seat.

In fact, he doesn't wear a stitch,
So he can scratch if there's an itch.

I hope that you don't find him rude—
My dog is happy in the nude.

—*Bruce Lansky*

## Consumer Price Duplex

Two can live as cheap as one;
I guess I always knew it.
But now it takes the two of us
To earn enough to do it.

—*Evelyn Amuedo Wade*

## Turnabout

If I'm so smart
Why aren't I rich?
I just don't have
Your greedy itch.
Let's put the horse
Before the cart:
If you're so rich
Why aren't you smart?

*—Hank Hill*

## To Have and Too Old

The bride, white of hair, is stooped over her cane,
  Her faltering footsteps need guiding,
While down on the church aisle, with a wan, toothless smile,
  The groom in a wheelchair comes riding.

And who is this elderly couple, you ask?
  You'll find, when you've closely explored it,
That here is that rare, most conservative pair,
  Who waited till they could afford it.

*—Richard Armour*

## Newspaper Headline: *Woman Gives Birth at Sixty-Five*

I thought that I would never see
A mom give birth at sixty-three.
Perhaps when she is sixty-four
She'll contemplate a couple more.
But if she waits till sixty-five
To let maternal instincts thrive,
She may just find it worth the wait,
'Cause Medicare may pay the freight.

—*Mae Scanlan*

# Money

Workers earn it,
Spendthrifts burn it,
Bankers lend it,
Women spend it,
Forgers fake it,
Taxes take it,
Dying leave it,
Heirs receive it,
Thrifty save it,
Misers crave it,
Robbers seize it,
Rich increase it,
Gamblers lose it . . .
I could use it.

—*Richard Armour*

## Money

That money talks
I won't deny.
I heard it once,
It said, "Goodbye."

—*Richard Armour*

## Oh Fudge!

Tonight before I hit the sack,
I'm going to have a little snack—
So if tomorrow I can't budge,
You'll know I've finished all the fudge.

—*Bruce Lansky*

## Snack Attack

We sneak another midnight snack
And think no one will know it;
But those who don't count calories
Have figures that will show it.

—*Charles Ghigna*

## Slimerick

A lady who dieted madly
Regarded her silhouette sadly,
    For the pounds she had lost
    At such strenuous cost
Were from right where she needed 'em badly.

—*Paul Humphrey*

## Side Effects

I'm worried about too much yoga.
Just what will I get for my pains?
If I stand on my head every morning
I'll end up with varicose brains.

—*Joan Van Poznak*

## Baldy Bean

I feel so bad for Uncle Ted.
There's not much hair upon his head.
And what is worse, he barely hears—
There's too much hair inside his ears.

—*Bruce Lansky*

## A Corny Story

As we grow older, year by year,
my husband always mourns.
The less and less we feel our oats,
the more we feel our corns.

—*Evelyn Amuedo Wade*

# It's Not the Fact

It's not the fact that all my hair
Is jumping ship in droves,
Or that I hoard my medicines
Like precious treasure troves.

It's not that once-true memory banks
Will not cooperate,
Or parts that once had muscle tone
Now downward gravitate.

It's not the fact that I can't eat
The food I used to love.
It's not a single one of these—
It's all of the above.

—*Robert Scotellaro*

## Over Thirty

Though I grow older, I'm aware
   That time can never floor me;
For middle age, like falling hair,
   Recedes each year before me.

Mirage-like it remains beyond
   The age at which I find me;
And, pacing this phenomenon,
   Youth closes in behind me.

From this is gleaned a useful truth
   And logical directive:
The secret of eternal youth
   Lies in a warped perspective.

—*Joyce La Mers*

## When Twenty Years Have Passed

Attend no class reunions
If respect you want to win.
Unless, of course, you're wealthy
Or you're famous, or you're thin.

—*Helen Ksypka*

## No Sweat

You know you're into middle age
When first you realize
That caution is the only thing
You care to exercise.

—*Charles Ghigna*

## Compensation

Like me, my love's not wrinkle-free.
His eyes, and mine, are growing dim.
And so he still looks good to me,
And I don't look so bad to him!

—*Nancy B. Chapman*

# Shakespeare Sonnet XVIII Revised

Shall I compare thee to a summer's day?
I'd like to, but thou'rt simply much too old.
Thy face is wrinkled, and thy hair is gray,
The years hang from thy frame like wads of mold.
A summer's day is jazzy, light of step,
A summer's day is ephemeral, and bright,
Whilst thou, my love, art hoary, without pep—
Best I compare thee to a winter's night.
But hold! A winter's night hath special charms
Undreamt of in the good old summertime,
And here within the haven of thine arms
Thy faint but warming fire I find sublime.
Old wizened man, I'll stick to thee like glue
Until the end, for I am winter, too.

—*Mae Scanlan*

## Waist Full Thoughts

Middle age is so much more
Than wrinkles on our faces;
It's when broad minds and narrow waists
Begin exchanging places.

*—Charles Ghigna*

## Crossing the Border

Senescence begins
And middle age ends
The day your descendants
Outnumber your friends.

—*Ogden Nash*

# In Extremis

I saw my toes the other day.
I hadn't looked at them for months.
Indeed, they might have passed away.
And yet they were my best friends once.
When I was small, I knew them well.
I counted on them up to ten
And put them in my mouth to tell
The larger from the lesser. Then
I loved them better than my ears,
My elbows, adenoids, and heart.
But with swelling of the years
We drifted, toes and I, apart.
Now, gnarled and pale, each said, *j'accuse!*—
I hid them quickly in my shoes.

*—John Updike*

# Methuselah

Methuselah ate what he found on his plate,
And never, as people do now,
Did he note the amount of the calorie count;
He ate it because it was chow.
He wasn't disturbed as at dinner he sat,
Devouring a roast or a pie,
to think it was lacking in granular fat
Or a couple of vitamins shy.
He cheerfully chewed each species of food,
Unmindful of troubles or fears
Lest his health might be hurt
By some fancy dessert;
And he lived over nine hundred years.

*—Anonymous*

# On the Vanity of Earthly Greatness

The tusks that clashed in mighty brawls
Of mastodons, are billiard balls.

The sword of Charlemagne the Just
Is ferric oxide, known as rust.

The grizzly bear whose potent hug
Was feared by all, is now a rug.

Great Caesar's bust is on the shelf,
And I don't feel so well myself.

*—Arthur Guiterman*

## Morning Ritual

I get up each morning
And dust off my wits,
Then pick up the paper
And read the obits.
If my name isn't there,
Then I know I'm not dead.
I eat a good breakfast
And go back to bed.

—*Anonymous*

## A Lesson Learned

One day, my skydiving Uncle Newt
Forgot to pack his parachute.
"That's one mistake," said Auntie Jen,
"That he will never make again."

—*Bruce Lansky*

## Waste

I had written to Aunt Maud,
Who was on a trip abroad,
When I heard she'd died of cramp.
Just too late to save the stamp.

—*Harry Graham*

# Graveside Advice

As I was lowered in my grave,
My mother yelled out, "Please behave."

Now mother is a little dense.
Her warning didn't make much sense.

I mean, I'm dead for goodness' sake.
What difference could behavior make?

On second thought, it's not so strange.
It's just that mothers never change.

—*Bruce Lansky*

## Time to Go

Please don't be sad,
If when you go,
You die without
A lot of dough.

For you will find,
When you are gone,
There isn't much
To spend it on.

—*Bruce Lansky*

# Gossips' End

When gossips die, as mortals must,
    And leave their earthly home,
Their punishment will be, I trust,
    Eternally to roam.

Down dismal paths and darkened pits
    And empty halls of hell,
With heads crammed full of juicy bits
    And not a soul to tell.

—*Richard Armour*

## The River Styx

While crossing the Styx I could tell
That the ferryman didn't fare well.
    He despairingly said,
    "All my clients are dead,
"And my business is going to hell."

—*Leslie Danford Perkins*

## Be Careful

Be careful of the words you say,
Keep them soft and sweet.
You'll never know from day to day
Which ones you'll have to eat.

—*Anonymous*

### Slight Mistake

So I took his horse
    And had it shot.
When I returned
    The Prince wailed, *"What?*
*Shot* my horse?
    You stupid clod!
I said to go and have it *shod!"*

—*William Rossa Cole*

## Ergo the Ego

Conversing with an egotist
Takes lots of concentration
Because you often find yourself
Me-deep in conversation.

—*Charles Ghigna*

# Predictable

As poor as a church mouse,
As strong as an ox,
As cute as a button,
As smart as a fox.

As thin as a toothpick,
As white as a ghost,
As fit as a fiddle,
As dumb as a post.

As bald as an eagle,
As neat as a pin,
As proud as a peacock,
As ugly as sin.

When people are talking,
You know what they'll say
As soon as you hear them
begin a cliché.

*—Bruce Lansky*

# An Attempt at Unrhymed Verse

People tell you all the time,
Poems do not have to rhyme;
It's often better if they don't,
And I'm determined this one won't.
                Oh dear.

Never mind, I'll start again,
Busy, busy with my pen . . . cil.
I can do it if I try—
Easy, peasy, pudding, and gherkins.

Writing verse is so much fun,
Cheering as the summer weather.
Makes you feel alert and bright,
'Specially when you get it more
    or less the way you want it.

—*Wendy Cope*

# From a Publisher
# to Desperate Poets

We don't solicit avant-garde
and don't encourage rhyme.
We shun the trite and will not bite
at graphic or sublime.

We cringe at poets deep in love—
no sentimental sap.
We give the boot to sweet and cute
or formulaic crap.

Reporting time is very slow;
we make no guarantee.
What's even worse, to read your verse,
we charge a healthy fee.

If published, we retain all rights
to print your precious baby.
Expecting pay? No way, José.
You'll get a copy—maybe.

*—Helen Ksypka*

## Pentagraph

I think. I think. I think. I think. I think.
Therefore, iamb.

—*Ed Conti*

## The Fool and the Poet

Sir, I admit your general rule,
That every poet is a fool,
But you yourself may serve to show it,
That every fool is not a poet.

—*Alexander Pope*

# The Hunter

The hunter crouches in his blind
'Neath camouflage of every kind,
And conjures up a quacking noise
To lend allure to his decoys.
This grown-up man, with pluck and luck,
Is hoping to outwit a duck.

—*Ogden Nash*

## A Fisherman's Prayer

Dear God, please let me catch a fish
So big that even I
When boasting of it afterwards
Will have no need to lie.

—*Anonymous*

## The Postman

Not gloom of night nor sodden ground
Stays him from his appointed round.
He slogs though rain and sleet and hail
To bring me someone else's mail.

—*Joyce La Mers*

# Postmaster: Handle with Care

Our mail person lately is cause for concern.
She's pregnant as any observer can learn
By merely a glance at her contour and size.
A short leave of absence would seem very wise.
When I see her coming I'm nudged by the fear
A Special Delivery may happen right here.

—*Irene Warsaw*

# Answering Machine Message

There's nobody home now
to answer the phone,
so please leave a message
when you hear the tone.

But if you're a burglar,
we're not gone at all—
we're cleaning our shotguns
while screening your call.

—*Mark Benthall*

# Is Anybody Home?

I used to grow old
When they put me on hold,
And I waited in silence, a martyr.
But the fashion today
Is to make music play,
And to soothe with a gentle sonata,
Or a silvery flute,
Or the song of a lute
Guaranteed to prevent me from groaning
As I glance at the clock.
Listen, don't give me Bach,
Give me simply the person I'm PHONING!

—*Maureen Cannon*

## The Inn Place

A restaurant nouvelle-cuisiny
Served fabulous quiche and linguine
    And six kinds of ices
    At à la carte prices
As high as the portions were teeny.

—*Bruce Bennett*

## Epitaph on a Waiter

By and by
God caught his eye.

—*David McCord*

## After the Philharmonic

Two paths diverged in a well-known park,
One well-lit, the other—dark.
And since I did not wish to die,
I took the one more traveled by.

*—James Camp*

## Space Age Saga

Travel is great, we depart from our home
    In a plane that zooms through the air.
With breakfast in Paris, and luncheon in Rome
    And luggage, alas, at O'Hare.

—*Evelyn Amuedo Wade*

## When in Dublin . . .

Drinking water from the Liffey
Is, to put it mildly, iffy.
My advice is, don't tempt fate:
In Dublin, drink your whiskey straight.

—*Charles W. Pratt*

## Literary Afterthought

Drink to me only with thine eyes,
And spare the dwindling gin supplies.

—*Mary Holtby*

## Song of the Open Road

I think that I shall never see
A billboard lovely as a tree.
Indeed, unless the billboards fall
I'll never see a tree at all.

*—Ogden Nash*

## Lather As You Go

Beneath this slab
John Brown is stowed.
He watched the ads,
And not the road.

—*Ogden Nash*

## George Washington Slept Everywhere

By innuendo, Washington has got
A most unsavory sort of reputation.
I guess you've got to sleep around a lot
To get to be the Father of a Nation.

—*Bob McKenty*

## Birds of a Feather

Of holidays and special days
November has its share—
Thanksgiving and Election Day
Are both located there.

Is it just coincidence,
Or can there be a reason,
That we select a president
When turkeys are in season?

—*Hannah Fox*

## The River Thames

Sailing on the river Thames
I said to Clyde, "Let's look for dames."
"It's called," said stuffy Clyde, "The Tems."
"OK," I said, "let's look for fems."

—*Edmund Conti*

## Deep Freeze

Siberia always
Seems to me
A very frigid
Place to be.
Surely Russians
Living there
Must wear thermal
Underwear.
But, of course,
I'm only guessing.
I've never seen
A Russian dressing.

—*Hank Hill*

## Horse Sense

Common sense is rare of course,
at any time, in any place.
That's the sense that keeps a horse
From betting on the human race.

—*Marcy S. Powell*

## Nearing the Finish

As I often remark when I'm low as can be,
    It's a terrible rat race I'm in,
And what is still worse, I'm beginning to see,
    The rats are quite likely to win.

—*Richard Armour*

# Eggomania

Consider the egg, it's a miracle,
    A thing so diverse for its size
That we hardly can help growing lyrical
    When given the Pullet Surprise.

The scope of this peerless comestible
    Must drive other foods to despair,
Since it's not only fully digestible
    But great for shampooing the hair.

It's boilable, poachable, fryable;
    It scrambles, it makes a sauce thicken;
It's also the only reliable
    Device for producing a chicken.

—*Felicia Lamport*

## Grace

God made the rooster,
　　God made the hen,
But Ma made the chicken
　　Pot pie. Amen!

—*J. Patrick Lewis*

## The Fly

God in His wisdom made the fly
And then forgot to tell us why.

—*Ogden Nash*

Our God, some contend, is immutable,
And their faith is, indeed, irrefutable:
    When He does what He should,
    It's because "He is good,"
When He doesn't, "His ways are inscrutable."

—*Laurence Perrine*

## Résumé

Razors pain you;
Rivers are damp;
Acids stain you;
And drugs cause cramp.
Guns aren't lawful;
Nooses give;
Gas smells awful;
You might as well live.

*—Dorothy Parker*

# Report After a Walk

To my wife. To the mailman.
To my neighbor next door.
To the affable druggist
And the clerk in his store.
To the gas-pump attendant.
To the chap who sells beer.
To the real-estate agent.
To the hardware cashier.
To the couple who run
The variety shop.
To the banker, the barber,
the jeweler, the cop.

Since I value your friendship,
I'm happy to say,
I did as you told me
And had a nice day.

*—Pyke Johnson, Jr.*

# Author Index

# Title Index

# Credits

Susan Anderson for "Midlife Muddle." © 1998 by Susan Anderson. Reprinted by permission of the author.

Alfred A. Knopf, Inc. for "In Extremis" from Collected Poems 1953-1993 by John Updike. Copyright © 1993 by John Updike. Reprinted by permission of Alfred A. Knopf, Inc.

Richard Armour for "Room Temperature," "Proof of the Puppy," "Watchdog," "Money," "Past Perfect," "Money," "Gossip's End," "Nearing the Finish," "Miniature," "Please Graduate," and "To Have and Too Old." © by Richard Armour. Reprinted by permission of Kathleen S. Armour for Richard Armour.

Bruce Bennett for "The Inn Place." © 1998 by Bruce Bennett. Reprinted by permission of the author.

Mark Benthall for "Answering Machine Message." © 1998 by Mark Benthall. Reprinted by permission of the author.

Bits Press for "After the Philharmonic" by James Camp. © 1978 by James Camp. Reprinted by permission of Bits Press.

Bits Press for "Birds of a Feather" by Hannah Fox. ©

## Other titles edited by Bruce Lansky

Humor books

*Age Happens*
*Familiarity Breeds Children*
*For Better And For Worse*
*Golf: It's Just a Game!*
*Laugh Twice and Call Me in the Morning*
*Lovesick*
*Work and Other Occupational Hazards*

Children's poetry books

*A Bad Case of the Giggles*
*Happy Birthday to Me!*
*Kids Pick the Funniest Poems*
*Miles of Smiles*
*No More Homework! No More Tests!*
*Poetry Party*

**To order, please call 1-800-338-2232**